Rocking Chair Puzzlers™

Brain Teasers

Bob Moog

spinner/books

Editorial Director: Melissa Fortunato
Designer: Jeanette Miller
Special thanks to Alexis Evans, Kristen Schoen, Connie Gee
and Lisa Choromanski for their invaluable assistance!

Printed in China.

ISBN 1-57561-227-5

TABLE OF CONTENTS

Introduction

The seeds of this book were planted several decades ago when my father, Alva Moog Jr., asked me if I wanted a piece of licorice. We were at my grandparents' house and Dad was sitting in Papa Percy's favorite chair. He smiled at me and said, "Bobby, just tell me one thing: 'What color was George Washington's white horse?'" I paused and reflected on the question. I was four years old and knew little about George Washington or breeds of horses. However, I was learning how to listen to a question carefully! Not only did I win the licorice, but I then challenged Dad with "Hey, guess what I'm holding in my empty hand?" My brainteaser career had started.

This book combines my favorite classic brainteasers, some new ones that I have created and a few special gems from my childhood banter with Dad.

I hope you enjoy solving them as much as my designer Jeanette Miller and I enjoyed creating them.

– Bob Moog

Precedent or President

Is it more likely that Peter Cannon is a historian or an economist if he thinks that

Abraham Lincoln is five times better than George Washington but four times worse than Andrew Jackson?

Alphabet Soup

What **three** letters can
be arranged to describe

a **beverage,**
a **verb**
and
a **homonym?**

The circle game

Geometry is hard for Silly Sally.

Which

is

BIGGER?

a square with a 1 foot side	or	**a circle with a 1 foot diameter?**

Paw Paw's Handyman

Quincy can paint a room in 6 hours.

Emmitt can paint the same room in 3 hours.

How long will it take if they are both painting?

Lost in Space

In what state would you find yourself
if you left St. Louis and went
five miles east, then 200 miles north
and then 40 miles west?

5 mi E ▷

200 mi N △

40 mi W ◁

over easy

Who am I?

I am a very fragile, rotund little man. I once had an accident that left me so disfigured that even the King of England and his fine staff failed at attempts to repair me.

Stand and Sign

Who am I?   **I am from Ohio and I served as both leader of my country in the early 20th century and as a justice of my country's highest court. Baseball is my favorite sport and I made my greatest contribution to the game when I got tired of sitting around $\frac{7}{9}$ of the way through a game.**

Wordly Wise

Alva's new Ford Fiesta was towed while sitting in front of this sign.

> **No Unauthorized Vehicles Will Be Towed**

Why did Alva go to court to fight the ticket? Why did Alva bring Mr. Smith, a local high school teacher, with him as his witness?

Food, Please

14

Napoleon's army was the first to use what food preservative device in combat?

Hint: Napoleon knew that "An army travels on its stomach."

Winter Construction

Lani's hands were freezing after building a snowman without any gloves. Should Lani warm up by putting her hands under cold water or hot water?

Most **Wanted** ?

Jeff

Harris

Sal

Al

In which state capitals will you find these guys?

No Blankety Blanks!

Look at the words below and see if you can complete the statement by filling in the blanks. A word hidden inside of each word listed below is needed to complete the sentence.

A. Panhandle
Spearmint
Aspirin

B. Wheeling
Germany
Washington

A. Meg stopped the _____ with a quick stab of the _____ that she held with her right _____ .

B. The _____ was really tired since the _____ weighed a _____ .

Light Show

What is the name of the toy

constructed by placing multiple

18 mirrors at different angles,

shooting light through

a tube bouncing the

light from one

mirror to the next?

Color Blind
Is it black, red or white?

1 **Major League Baseball umpire's underwear**

2 **A Catholic novice's garb**

3 **Archie Andrew's hair**

4 **Stitching on a baseball**

5 **Wimbledon tennis players' dress code**

Family Matters

True   False

In 14 states, including Utah, it
is legal for a man to
marry his widow's sister.

Dog Dayz

What is the

next letter

in this series?

D N O S A J

Just Kidding

"Let's go play with the 3 kids up on that hill," said Silly Sally. Joe ran ahead but only found 2 children and some grazing farm animals when he arrived. Where did the third kid go?

Buried Treasure

Is it against the law to bury a person in Utah who is permanently living in Nevada?

Go West, Young Woman

N

W

E

S

Erin left New York and flew to California. The flight took five hours. If Erin left at 11:00am, when did she arrive?

I am
C·O·U·N·T·I·N·G
on you

What number is

ONE

more than TEN HUNDRED

and one?

1001001

All in
the Family

Try to name the three

most closely related

pairs of presidents.

Hysterical History

Did the Germans
bomb Pearl Harbor
on December 7th

1941,

1942

or

1944?

Sister Sprinters

Nina and Lydia start from their home and each run 2 miles. Nina can run a mile in 8 minutes 30 seconds and Lydia can run a mile in 9 minutes 10 seconds. When they finish running, what is the farthest apart they can be?

Sunrise, Sunset

can't be found at noon

What starts today,

and is required to end sunset?

Digestive Detective

Jeff and Vinnie met for dinner at Fitz's Fine Foods.

After they both went to the bathroom they sat down and ordered. The waiter described the special as trout almondine with asparagus covered in hollandaise sauce. Jeff said, "I'll take it, but Vinnie wants something else. He had asparagus for lunch."

How did Jeff know what Vinnie had for lunch?

3 Men
and a Lady

Melissa went to dinner with

Andrew,

George

and

Ulysses,

but she ate **alone**.

Not surprisingly, they all showed up
to pay for her meal.

Why?

Can YOU canoe?

TWO fathers and TWO sons went on a canoe trip,

ONE fell out

and TWO were left.

Where is the 4th man?

Hi Ho Silver

Ben Cartwright rode into Virginia City late on Friday. Ben Cartwright stayed two days, but still rode out on Friday.

33

Explain.

It's Not Over -Till It's Over

Andrew and John are professional tennis players who never like to lose. They were 9/10 of the way through a game with John down by 3 points. Andrew made a very good shot. Then, without giving John a chance, Andrew made another good shot. John suspected that he was going to lose, even though the game wasn't over. Why?

Coin - cidentally

Miss Korn collected coins and referred
to her coin collection by nicknames.

Her pennies were the Cu collection;
her nickels were the Ni collection.
What did Miss Korn call her
collection of silver dollars?

Phractured Phrases

Try to identify the two words we replaced
in these well-known quotes below:

"What is good for the stomach is
good for the complexion."

"In this world nothing is certain
but franks and beans."

"You're either part of the infield
or part of the outfield."

"The only thing we have to drink is beer itself."

Road Trip

Which state capitals would you visit to find a . . .

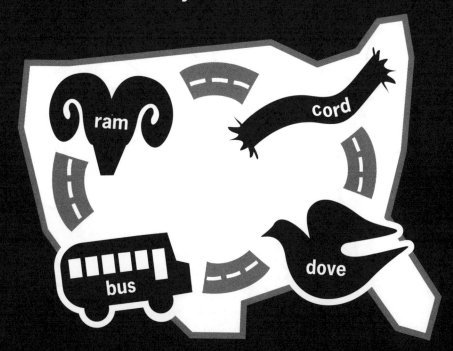

ram

cord

bus

dove

Talking States

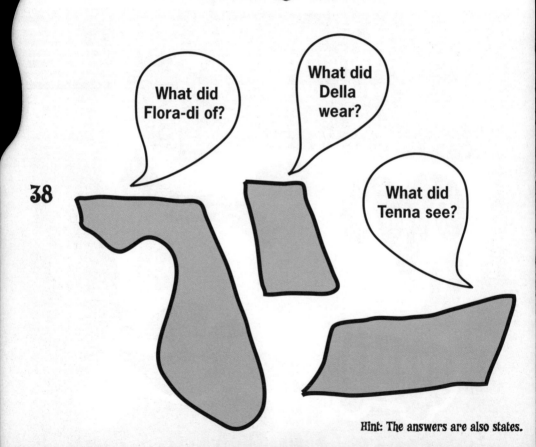

Hint: The answers are also states.

Sheila the GREAT

Sheila lives in Chicago. One night she sat down for dinner with the window open and heard a gunshot. Then she witnessed two gruesome deaths. Before she could leave the room she saw a building catch fire. Why didn't Sheila call the police?

Wait Until Dark

Jacob and Lutz were camping in June. Before going to sleep, they decided to read a book. They both agreed to stop reading when it got dark. They were not fast readers, but they both finished the entire encyclopedia. How?

Nuts to you

1. What is the largest nut?

2. What is a policeman's favorite nut?

3. What is another name for a sneeze nut?

Drink Up

What city in Thailand would you visit to order an original Singapore Sling?

A Bush in the Hand

Would you be more likely to find
2 bushes and no trees at...

the
White House
lawn,

or

the
Supreme Court
building?

Disneyland

Boy

Jupiter Jones won a contest where first prize was "use of a Rolls Royce with chauffeur for 30 days of 24 hours each." He used the limousine on June 1, 2 and 3, for 8 hours each day. He then used it again from June 12 to June 19 for 8 hours each day. When Jupiter arrived to take the limo on July 2 he was told that his 30 days were up. Why did Jupiter disagree and how many days did he think were left?

1st PRIZE

Sunny and Fair

Who am I?

I am a singer who has had hits
in five consecutive decades.
I also have won an Academy Award.
I am as well-known for my
Bob Mackie dresses as I am for
my songs. In 2003, I began my
"farewell" concert tour.

Down Under

Shane bet Steve that it was impossible to go back in time.

Why did Shane agree that Steve won the bet when their plane arrived in Los Angeles, California from Adelaide, Australia?

Double Trouble

Pacific Ocean

Atlantic Ocean

In what U.S. city
can you visit a state capital,
see the Atlantic Ocean, drive an
hour to the Pacific Ocean and see
17th-century architecture?

Birthday Boy

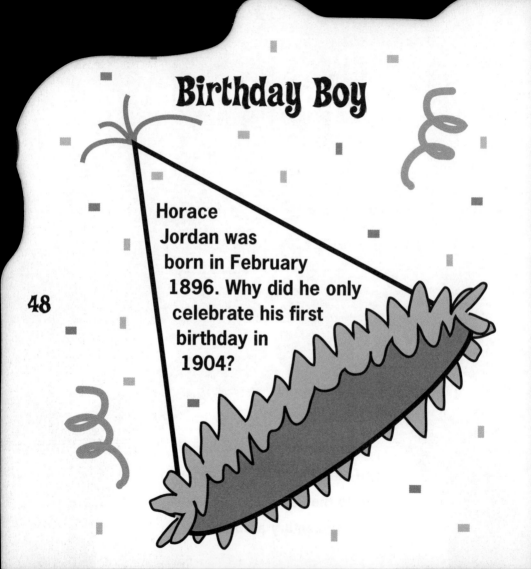

Horace Jordan was born in February 1896. Why did he only celebrate his first birthday in 1904?

Shoe Who?

Silly Sally was so excited to fly from San Francisco to London that she forgot how sore her new shoes made her feet. She took her shoes off as soon as she was settled in her seat. When the plane landed 10 hours later, Sally started screaming at the flight attendant when she realized that her shoes had shrunk.

Explain.

Time to Go

Mr. Rosner walked into the room and noticed Silly Sally sitting patiently on the floor reading a magazine. Mr. Rosner's alarm clock was totally destroyed and parts were all over the room. What had Silly Sally been up to?

Friend or Fiend?

If Billy the Brat told Silly Sally

"I hate you,

I loathe you,

I despise you,"

would he be a practitioner of

hyperbole,
redundancy or
immaturity?

Forgotten Children

Homer's mother has four children.

Three of them are named
Spring,
Summer
and
Autumn.

What is the
fourth named?

Epitome

Jeff Glik is camping outside Bemidji, Minnesota with only oil lamps, a candle and some birch bark. He has only one match. Which should he light first?

53

BUS STOP

If 50 kids fit in a school bus, how many buses do you need to get 125 kids to school?

Happy Birthday, Granny

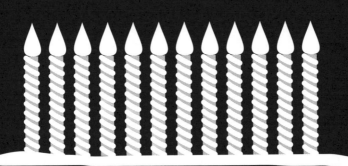

Claudia and her 52-year-old mother went to her grandmother's 50th birthday party together. How can Claudia's grandmother be younger than Claudia's mother?

Wide Load

Mr. Stone's truck attempted to enter a parking garage, but got caught underneath the garage ceiling because of the truck's 6'6" height. It won't budge forward or backward. How can he get the truck out from under the garage ceiling?

Compass Confusion

N

One summer morning Emily decided to drive from her favorite casino in Reno, Nevada to visit her mom in Los Angeles, California. Did Emily travel east or west?

S

W

E

Cassie's Classic Conundrum

Using the digits 1 through 9, number the squares
below so the sum of all the squares vertically,
horizontally and diagonally is always 15.

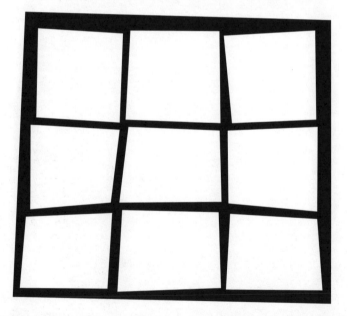

(By the way, you can only use each number one time.)

Desperate Date

Name the European cities where Silly Sally went to find the following boys:

Don

Lin

Bud

Ari

(Hint: She went to Toronto to find Ron.)

Phone Tree

Maia wants to call all 10 kids in her 6th grade class

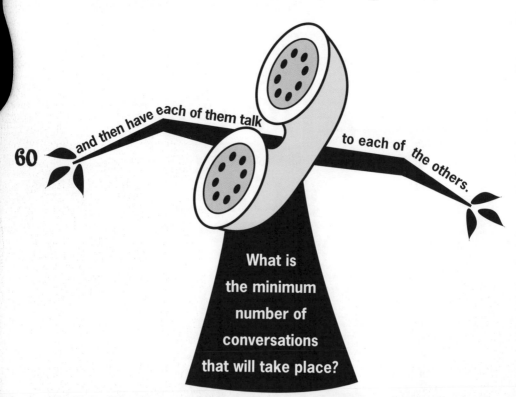

and then have each of them talk to each of the others.

60

What is the minimum number of conversations that will take place?

Fractional

Sense

How much is
30 divided by
½ plus 3?

How do you
represent the
number 50 in base 5?

Busybody

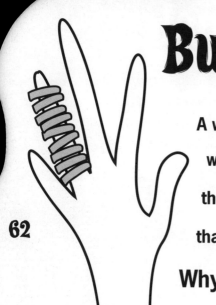

A woman married **over 50 men** without ever getting divorced. None of the men died and no one thought that she acted improperly.

Why?

62

E-X-T-R-A
Credit

What two European cities
would you visit to find
Ed and Sara?

What do the following birds have in common?

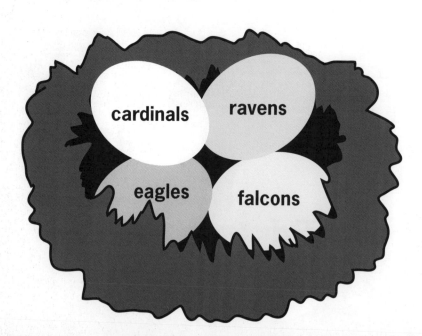

cardinals

ravens

eagles

falcons

If I Ran the ZOO

In what northern

hemisphere city

can you find

indigenous

tigers and lions?

No Blankety Blanks!

Look at the words below and see if you can complete the statement by filling in the blanks. A word hidden inside of each place listed below is needed to complete the sentence.

Broadway
Oregon
Kentucky
Frankfort
Colorado

The _____ of the _____ sent _____ and

_____ on the wrong _____ .

Time is **UP**

I like time,
    but I don't like clocks.

I like wine,
    but I don't like beer.

I like Cherie,
    but I don't like Jenny.

Do I like George, Bob or Mark?

OUT of ink

Rotten Robbie went into Mike's Magic Shop and bought $100 worth of magic tricks and magic books. Robbie signed a personal check and left the store. After he left, Mike looked at the check and was surprised to see that it wasn't signed. What happened?

Answers

Precedent or President

An economist. Peter thinks of U.S. dollars when he thinks of these presidents.

Washington = $1, Lincoln = $5, Jackson = $20

Alphabet Soup

e, t, a: tea (beverage), eat (verb), ate (homonym)

The Circle Game

A square has a larger area, since the circle with a 1-foot diameter will actually fit inside a square with a 1-foot side.

Paw-Paws Handyman

2 hours (Emmitt can paint 1/3 of the room in an hour while Quincy can paint 1/6 of the room in an hour. In 2 hours they will paint $2/3 + 2/6 = 1$ entire painted room.)

Lost in Space

State of confusion! More likely close to Burlington, Iowa.

Over Easy

Humpty Dumpty.

Stand and Sign

William H. Taft started the tradition of the 7th inning stretch. He also is the only man to become Chief Justice of the Supreme Court after his presidency (1909-1913).

Wordly Wise

Without a period after the word "vehicles," the sign clearly told Alva that his car would not be towed. Mr. Smith, a high school English teacher, cleared up the grammar issues for the judge. Alva had a good case and won in traffic court.

Food, Please

The tin can (This allowed armies to travel longer distances without having to search for farmers who could feed them. Fresh food spoiled after a few days, but the new canned rations kept Napoleon's army marching for weeks at a time.)

Winter Construction

Cold water (She wouldn't feel how hot the hot water is and could burn herself badly.)

Most Wanted

Jeff (Jefferson City, MO)
Harris (Harrisburg, PA)
Sal (Salem, OR)
Al (Albany, NY)

No Blankety Blanks

A. Pan<u>handle</u> B. <u>Wheel</u>ing
   <u>Spear</u>mint   Ger<u>man</u>y
   <u>Asp</u>irin   Washing<u>ton</u>

A. Meg stopped the <u>asp</u> with a quick stab of the <u>spear</u>
  that she held with her right <u>hand</u>.
B. The <u>man</u> was really tired since the <u>wheel</u> weighed a <u>ton</u>.

Light Show

A kaleidoscope.

Color Blind

Major League Baseball umpire's underwear (black)
A Catholic novice's garb (white)
Archie Andrew's hair (red)
Stitching on a baseball (red)
Wimbledon tennis players' dress code (white)

Family Matters

False. If he has a widow, he is dead.

Dog Dayz

J (June-the letters are tied to the first letter of the month of the year.)

Just Kidding

The third kid was a baby goat.

Buried Treasure

Yes. (You can't bury living people.)

Go West, Young Woman

1:00 pm. (There is a three-hour time difference.)

I am Counting on You

One thousand (ten hundred) and two, 1002.

All in the Family

John Adams (father) - John Quincy Adams (son)
George H. Bush (father) - George W. Bush (son)
William H. Harrison (grandfather) - Benjamin Harrison (grandson)

Hysterical History

The Germans didn't bomb Pearl Harbor, the Japanese did (in 1941).

Sister Sprinters

Four miles. (They ran in opposite directions.)

Sunrise, Sunset

The letter "t."

Digestive Detective

When they went to the bathroom, Jeff noticed that Vinnie's urine was green (and smelly too!). Jeff's deductive reasoning told him that the source of the color was a recent experience with asparagus.

3 Men and a Lady

Mr. George Washington, Mr. Andrew Jackson and Mr. Ulysses S. Grant are paper money. Her meal cost $71 with gratuity. Washington is on the $1 bill, Jackson is pictured on the $20 bill and Grant is on the $50 bill.

Can You Canoe?

He doesn't exist. A grandfather, father and son got into the canoe and the son fell out, leaving the grandfather and the father… who is also a son.

Hi Ho Silver

Friday was the name of Ben's horse.

It's Not Over - Till it's Over

They were bowling and Andrew made two strikes in the 10th frame, putting him ahead by 23 points with one shot remaining. John doubted he could do better.

Coin-cidentally

The Ag collection. (Her nicknames come from the symbols on the Periodic Chart. Cu is copper, Ni is nickel and Ag is Silver.)

Phractured Phrases

"What is good for the <u>goose</u> is good for the <u>gander</u>."
–English proverb

"In this world nothing is certain but <u>death</u> and <u>taxes</u>."
–Benjamin Franklin, letter to M. Leroy, 1789

"You're either part of the <u>solution</u> or part of the <u>problem</u>."
–Eldridge Cleaver

"The only thing we have to <u>fear</u> is <u>fear</u> itself."
–Franklin D. Roosevelt, Inaugural Address, 1933

Road Trip

Sac<u>ram</u>ento, CA; Colum<u>bus</u>, OH; Con<u>cord</u>, NH;
<u>Dover</u>, DE

Talking States

She died of Missouri.
She wore her New Jersey.
Ida no, but Alaska.

Sheila the <u>Great</u>

Sheila was watching television.

Wait Until Dark

They were in Lapland, land of the midnight sun, and the
sun didn't set until September.

Nuts to You

1. Coconut
2. Doughnut
3. Cashew

Drink Up

None. (Singapore isn't in Thailand. You would go to the Raffles Hotel in Singapore.)

A Bush in the Hand

White House lawn. (Presidents Bush.)

Calendar Boy

Since all days have 24 hours, Jupiter reasoned that the rationale for specifying the number of hours in a day was to define what a day was. By his calculations, he had only used the limo 80 hours or three days and eight hours. He contended that he still had use of the limo for another 26 days and 16 hours.

Sunny and Fair

Cher.

Down Under

South Australia is 18 hours ahead of California. They left on Tuesday at 3:00 p.m. California time and their flight took 15 hours total, so they arrived before they left.

Double Trouble

Salem is the name of a U.S. city in Massachusetts and Oregon. Portland is an incorrect answer since it does not have 17th-century architecture.

Birthday Boy

He was born on February 29th. 1904 was the first leap year after 1896. Normally every four years there is a leap year, but there was no leap year in 1900.

Shoe Who?

Sally's feet had swelled from the change in compression in the plane and the hours of sitting without getting proper circulation in her feet.

Time to Go

She was just killing time while she waited for Mr. Rosner, her little lambchop.

Friend or Fiend

Probably all three! Hyperbole is gross exaggeration, redundancy is repeating oneself and immaturity is always in character for Billy.

Forgotten Children

Homer. (Of course!)

Epitome

The match.

Bus Stop

3 buses. (Each bus holds 50 kids, so two buses hold 100 kids and the third is needed for the extra 25.)

Happy Birthday, Granny

Claudia's father is 32 and his mother was 18 when he was born.

Wide Load

Let air out of the tires. (The truck will lower and be able to drive forward.)

Compass Confusion

East. (Los Angeles is actually east of Reno.)

Cassie's Classic Conundrum

8	1	6
3	5	7
4	9	2

Desperate Date

London
Berlin
Budapest
Paris

Phone Tree

45 individual conversations. The formula is $\frac{N(n-1)}{2}$, where N is the total number of kids. So $10(10-1) \div 2 = 45$. Another way to do it is to say Maia talked to nine, the next kid talked to eight and add up all the conversations.

Fractional Sense

63 (30 ÷ 1/2 = 60, 60 + 3 = 63)

100 (In base 5, the number 5 is 10, the number 15 is 20.
To express 50, which is 10 groups of 5, the correct
number is 100.)

Busybody

She was a Justice of the Peace.

Extra Credit

<u>Edi</u>nburg and <u>Sara</u>jevo.

Chirp Chirp

They are all NFL team names.

If I Ran the Zoo

Detroit, MI (home of the Detroit Tigers and the Detroit Lions).

No Blankety Blanks!

The <u>color</u> of the <u>ore</u> sent <u>Ken</u> and <u>Frank</u> on the wrong <u>road</u>.

<u>Colora</u>do
<u>Ore</u>gon
<u>Ken</u>tucky
<u>Frank</u>fort
<u>Broad</u>way

Time is Up

George. (I only like things that end with the letter "e".)

Out of ink

Robbie used a pen with disappearing ink. That's why he is so rotten.

About the Author

Bob Moog, co-founder of University Games and publisher of Spinner Books, has been creating brainteasers since childhood. He tormented his four younger siblings with quizzes, conundrums and physical and mental challenges during the 1960s. Now he introduces the Rocking Chair Puzzlers™ series, hoping it will challenge and puzzle you as much as they confounded the Moog children 40 years ago.

Bob Moog is the author of several other puzzle, game and children's books, including: *Gummy Bear Goes to Camp*, *20 Questions*, *30 Second Mysteries* and *Truth or Dare*.